The Fire of Invention, the Fuel of Interest

The Fire of Invention, the Fuel of Interest

On Intellectual Property

Michael Novak

The AEI Press

Publisher for the *American Enterprise Institute*

WASHINGTON, D.C.

1996

Available in the United States from the AEI Press, c/o Publisher Resources Inc., 1224 Heil Quaker Blvd., P.O. Box 7001, La Vergne, TN 37086-7001. Distributed outside the United States by arrangement with Eurospan, 3 Henrietta Street, London WC2E 8LU England.

ISBN 0-8447-7081-7

1 3 5 7 9 10 8 6 4 2

The AEI Press
Publisher for the American Enterprise Institute
1150 17th Street, N.W., Washington, D.C. 20036

Printed in the United States of America

Contents

Preface

In the summer of 1995, representatives of Pfizer Inc. approached me about preparing three lectures on key issues facing business corporations as the new century approaches. Although I was at first hesitant to set aside a book project already begun, the freedom I had to choose topics and approach led me to return to terrain I had first explored in the 1980s on the nature of the corporation in *The Corporation: A Theoretical Inquiry* and *Toward a Theology of the Corporation*.

Much has changed in the intervening years. A renewed account of the corporation seemed useful: what the corporation is, its new moral challenges and the new enemies it faces, and what goods (and dangers) it brings with it. This monograph on the nature of intellectual property and human creativity is the second in a series of three Pfizer Lectures, the first of which—on the future of the corporation—AEI recently published. The third lecture will explore crucial problems of corporate governance.

I would like to thank Pfizer Inc. for its support, and in particular Terry Gallagher and Carson Daly. In my own office, Cathie Love and Brian Anderson carried on with their usual competence and unusual good cheer; and the help of Cain Pence as a summer intern was indispensable. Permit me to thank AEI, too, which under the watchful eye of Chris DeMuth continues to provide a remarkably welcome home for research and writing; Isabel Ferguson and Ethel Dailey in the office of Seminars and Conferences, who arranged the public presentation on September 24, 1996; and Dana Lane, who showed her usual care in the supervision of this publication.

The Fire of Invention, the Fuel of Interest

On a cold winter day in February 1859, in Jacksonville, Illinois, Abraham Lincoln delivered a "Lecture on Discoveries and Inventions," in which he described, since the time of Adam, six great steps in the history of liberty. The last of these great steps, Lincoln held, is the law of copyrights and patents. His lecture gives the best account I have ever read of the reasons why the United States, in a brief Constitution of barely 4,486 words, includes a clause guaranteeing the "right" of inventors and authors to royalties for patents and copyrights (the single mention of the term *right* in the body of the Constitution). Until I read Lincoln on this point, I had never encountered anyone who gave patents and copyrights such high importance.

On that cold February day on the Illinois prairie, you must imagine Lincoln, tall and gangling, gazing across the stove-heated room, with a sweep of his hand summoning up a vision of that first "old fogy," father Adam:

There he stood, a very perfect physical man,
as poets and painters inform us; but he must
have been very ignorant, and simple in his
habits. He had no sufficient time to learn
much by observation; and he had no near
neighbors to teach him anything. No part
of his breakfast had been brought from the
other side of the world; and it is quite prob-
able, he had no conception of the world having any other side.[1]

By contrast with this naked but imposing Adam, able
to speak (for he names the animals) but without anyone to talk to (for Eve "was still a bone in his side"),
Young America, Lincoln notes, the America of 1859,
is awash with knowledge and wealth. Whereas the
first beautiful specimen of the species knows not how
to read or write, nor any of the useful arts yet to be
discovered, "Look around at Young America," Lincoln says in 1859. "Look at his apparel, and you shall
see cotton fabrics from Manchester and Lowell; flax-
linen from Ireland; wool-cloth from Spain; silk from
France; furs from the Arctic regions, with a buffalo
robe from the Rocky Mountains." On Young
America's table, one can find

> besides plain bread and meat made at home
> . . . sugar from Louisiana; coffee and fruits
> from the tropics; salt from Turk's Island; fish
> from New-foundland; tea from China, and
> spices from the Indies. The whale of the Pa-
> cific furnishes his candle-light; he has a dia-
> mond-ring from Brazil; a gold-watch from

California, and a spanish cigar from Havanna.

Not only does Young America have a sufficient, indeed more than sufficient, supply of these goods, but, Lincoln adds, "thousands of hands are engaged in producing fresh supplies, and other thousands, in bringing them to him."

The Grand Historical Adventure

Here, then, is the question Lincoln poses: How did the world get from the unlettered, untutored backwoodsman of the almost silent and primeval Garden of Eden to great cities, locomotives, telegraphs, and breakfast from across the seas? He discerns six crucial steps in this grand historical adventure.

The first step was God-given: the human ability to build a language.

The second step was the slow mastering of the art of discovery, through learning three crucial human habits—observation, reflection, and experiment—which Lincoln explains this way:

It is quite certain that ever since water has been boiled in covered vessels, men have seen the lids of the vessels rise and fall a little, with a sort of fluttering motion, by force of the steam; but so long as this was not specially observed, and reflected and experimented upon, it came to nothing. At length however, after many thousand years, some man observes this long-known effect of hot water lifting a pot-lid, and begins a train of reflection upon it.

Given how arduous it is to lift heavy objects, the attentive man is invited to experiment with the force lifting up the pot lid.

Thousands of years, however, were needed to develop the habit of observing, reflecting, and experimenting and then to spread that art throughout society. Some societies develop that habit socially, and some do not. Why, Lincoln asked, when Indians and Mexicans trod over the gold of California for centuries without finding it, did Yankees almost instantly discover it? (The Indians had not failed to discover it in South America.) "Goldmines are not the only mines overlooked in the same way," Lincoln noted. Indeed, there are more "mines" to be found above the surface of the earth than below: "All nature—the whole world, material, moral, and intellectual—is a mine; and, in Adam's day, it was a wholly unexplored mine." And so "it was the destined work of Adam's race to develop, by discoveries, inventions, and improvements, the hidden treasures of this mine."[2]

The third great step was the invention of writing. By this great step, taken only in a few places, spreading slowly, observations and reflections made in one century prompted reflection and experimentation in a later one.

The fourth great step was the printing press, which diffused records of observations, reflections, and experiments in ever-widening circles, far beyond the tiny handful of people who could afford handwritten parchment. Now such records could be made available to hundreds of thousands cheaply. Before printing, the great mass of humans

> were utterly unconscious, that their *conditions*, or their *minds* were capable of improvement. They not only looked upon the educated few as superior beings; but they supposed themselves to be naturally incapable of rising to equality. To immancipate [sic] the mind from this false and under estimate of itself, is the great task which printing came into the world to perform. It is difficult for us, *now* and *here*, to conceive how strong this slavery of the mind was; and how long it did, of necessity, take, to break it's [sic] shackles, and to get a habit of freedom of thought, established.

Between the invention of writing and the invention of the printing press, almost three thousand years had intervened. Between the invention of the printing press and the invention of a modern patent law (in Britain in 1624), less than two hundred.

The fifth great step was the discovery of America. In the new country, committed to liberty and equality, the human mind was emancipated as never before. Given a brand-new start, calling for new habits, "a new country is most favorable—almost necessary—to the immancipation of thought, and the consequent advancement of civilization and the arts." The discovery of America was "an event greatly facilitating useful discoveries and inventions."

The sixth great step was the adoption of a Constitution, in which the word *right* occurs only once, and that in Article 1, section 8, clause 8—the recognition of a natural right of authors and inventors. Among the few express powers granted by the people to Congress, the framers inserted this one:

> To promote the Progress of Science and useful Arts, by securing for limited Times to Authors and Inventors the exclusive Right to their respective Writings and Discoveries.

The effect of this regime was not lost upon the young inventor and future president.

"Before then," Lincoln wrote, "any man might instantly use what another had invented; so that the inventor had no special advantage from his own invention." Lincoln cuts to the essential: "The patent system changed this; secured to the inventor, for a limited time, the exclusive use of his invention; and thereby added the fuel of *interest* to the *fire* of genius, in the discovery and production of new and useful things."

"The fuel of *interest* added to the *fire* of genius!" Ever the realist, Lincoln knew what is in the human being: to be a genius is one thing, to be motivated is quite another, and then to be supported in this motivation by a wise regime is an unprecedented blessing. By contrast, a regime that does not secure natural rights depresses human energy.[3] Natural rights are not mere legal puffs of air; they formalize capacities for action that in some societies lie dormant and in others are fueled into ignition.

The United States, Lincoln believed, lit a fire to the practical genius of its people, among the high born and the low born alike, wherever God in his wisdom had implanted it. In the same year as his lecture, 1859, Lincoln himself won a U.S. patent, number 6469, for a "device to buoy vessels over shoals." That patent is not a bad metaphor for the effect of patents on inventions: to buoy them over difficulties.

The great effect of the patent and copyright clause on world history was a remarkable transvaluation of values. During most of human history, *land* had been the most important source of wealth; in America, *intellect* and *know-how* became the major source. The dynamism of the system ceased to be primarily material and became, so to speak, intellectual and spiritual, born of the creative mind. Lincoln's motive in favoring the Homestead Act and the patent clause (and both together) was to prevent the West from being dominated by large estates and great landowners, so that it might become a society of many freemen and many practical, inventive minds. And so it has. More than 5 million patents have been issued in the United States since the first patent law of 1790.[4]

From Lincoln to John Paul II

Implicit in Lincoln's Jacksonville lecture are several assumptions about the nature and meaning of the universe. Lincoln saw history as a narrative of freedom. He believed devoutly that the Creator of all things had made human beings in his own image—every one of them, woman and man—to be provident. History, he thought, is the record of how human beings have gradually come to recognize their true better nature and striven to make it actual, both in their own lives and in the institutions of their republic.

Thomas Jefferson wrote that "the God who gave us life gave us liberty,"[5] and, while Lincoln did not actually say that our God wishes to be adored by men who are free, he sacrificed much, very much, so that in 1861–1865 this nation might have "a new birth of freedom." That horrifying bloody project, he held— 40,000 dead and wounded in a single day (and more than once)—was willed by God. The universe is so created that it positively calls forth human freedom. To that call, it is the sacred duty of humans to respond, even at enormous cost.

Some seven score and two years after Lincoln's lecture in Jacksonville, there came an international echo of his beliefs from an unlikely quarter, in a world-wide letter published by Pope John Paul II in Rome, on May 1, 1991, *Centesimus Annus*. I do not know how much of Lincoln Pope John Paul II has read, but there is no mistaking the Lincolnian wavelength on which the papal letter on political economy traveled. His mind sweeping history like Lincoln's, and noting that for thousands of years *land* was the primary form of wealth, the pope writes: "In our time, in particular, there exists another form of ownership which is becoming no less important than land: *the possession of know-how, technology and skill.*" The wealth of the world's most economically advanced nations is based far more on this type of ownership than on natural resources.

"Indeed, besides the earth," observes the pope, "man's principal resource is *man himself*. His intelligence enables him to discover the earth's productive potential and the many different ways in which human needs can be satisfied." The pope's words seem cousin to Lincoln's sentence, "All nature—the whole world, material, moral, and intellectual—is a mine," and "the destiny of Adam's race" is "to develop, by discoveries, inventions, and improvements, the hidden treasures of this mine."

This thought is picked up later by the pope:

Whereas at one time the decisive factor of production was *the land*, and later capital—understood as a total complex of the instruments of production—today the decisive factor is increasingly *man himself*, that is, his knowledge, especially his scientific knowledge, his capacity for interrelated and compact organization, as well as his ability to perceive the needs of others and to satisfy them.[6]

Similarly, where Lincoln had written "but Adam had nothing to turn his attention to [but] work. If he should do anything in the way of invention, he had first to invent the art of invention," the pope writes:

At one time *the natural fruitfulness of the earth* appeared to be, and was in fact, the primary factor of wealth, while work was, as it were, the help and support for this fruitfulness. In our time . . . work becomes ever more fruitful and productive to the extent that people become more knowledgeable about the pro-

ductive potentialities of the earth and more
profoundly cognizant of the needs of those
for whom their work is done.[7]

Washington, Madison, and Lincoln held that the
American regime, measured by "the Laws of Nature
and Nature's God," would blaze a trail for other nations. Under Pope John Paul II, important portions
of its "new science of politics," after much testing,
have at last been ratified by what is now the most
widely held body of social thought in the world.[8] In
the coming third millennium, this practical intellectual influence may stand as an important contribu-
tion of American civilization to world history.

In this new era, observes Fred Warshofsky, a jour-
nalist-historian: "Creativity, in the form of ideas, innovations, and inventions, has replaced gold, colo-
nies, and raw materials as the new wealth of nations."
The remarkable "new technologies, new processes,
and new products that constitute intellectual property now form the economic bedrock of international
trade and national wealth."[9] As more and more nations take halting steps on the path of democracy and
free markets, they will increasingly need the fire of
invention, the fuel of interest.

Some Clarifications

Having sketched the theological horizon within
which the law of patents and copyrights functions in
world history, we must now come down to practical
questions. First, a clarification: the concepts of *copyright* and *patent* are not the same and have separate
histories. The early and somewhat shadowy origins

of the first tentative laws of patents lie in seventeenth-century Britain and in Germany and France; but these were often in the form of "grants of privilege," of monopoly or favor, awarded by the crown.

As Lincoln noted, the invention of the printing press in 1456 forced the issue of copyright on the attention of authors and philosophers, notably (in the English world) Hobbes and Locke. To the monarchs, copyright laws had early commended themselves as a means of censorship; but against this, philosophers and poets (like John Milton) soon enough rebelled. In addition, writers and inventors came increasingly from the lower ranks, from persons not of noble birth, who had no inheritance to prop them up, and were dependent on their wits for their livelihood. They wanted financial independence from printers, publishers, church, and crown.

In the United States, under the leadership of General Charles Pinckney of the South Carolina state legislature, that state put in place a law protecting the patents of inventors in 1784. The year before, 1783, under the leadership of James Madison, Virginia had already passed a law protecting the copyright of authors. These two events may explain why at the Constitutional Convention (on Saturday, August 18, 1787), Pinckney submitted a minute to the drafting committee urging the inclusion of a clause protecting patent rights, while on the same day Madison submitted another protecting copyrights.[10] Apparently, there was little serious debate; by 1787, all the states except Delaware had adopted similar legislation, and all the delegates were intent on promoting the sciences and useful arts in the infant republic as a whole. Both minutes were usefully combined in a single clause and given a place of honor among the enumerated powers in Article I.

By the time of the U.S. Constitution, the rooting of copyright in the common law and natural rights was already beyond dispute.[11] U.S. laws, however, clarified that the right inhered in the individual creator, not in the state, and is not a privilege or favor extended by the legislature. The law, instead, was regarded as securing a preexisting right (as the general verb used in the Declaration of Independence, "to secure these rights," clearly expresses). Thus, only in America were patent and copyright laws given constitutional status, and only here, for several generations, were they widely and popularly appealed to by rich and poor alike.

Now for the definitions. *Copyright*, literally, is a right to make copies, and a *patent* is a right to own royalties to a novel product or a novel process. Copyrights protect the creations of writers and artists, whereas patents protect the inventions and discoveries of inventors. Paul Goldstein of Stanford puts it quite succinctly: "Copyright is the law of authorship and patent is the law of invention." He adds:

> Copyright protects products of the human mind, the thoughts and expressions that one day may be found on the pages of a book and the next in a song or motion picture . . . . Patent law's domain is invention and technology, the work that goes into creating new products, whether tractors, pharmaceuticals, or electric can openers. The United States

Patent Act gives an inventor, or the company to which he has assigned his rights, the right to stop others from manufacturing, selling, or using an invention without the patent holder's permission.[12]

Not everyone accepts this concept. The philosopher Tom G. Palmer, for example, denies that there can be property ownership in ideas; ideas are "ideal objects," he says, quite different in their characteristics from material things.[13] But Palmer does not do justice to a crucial point: patent and copyright laws do not protect ideas or concepts, considered in their immateriality and shareability. On the contrary, copyright laws protect the concrete expression of ideas, their incarnation in the precise particulars of language and song singled out by their creators. Similarly, patent laws protect the concrete reduction to physical practice of practical insights. In both cases, it is not the general idea that is protected but the concrete incarnation.

For one to obtain a copyright, for example, it is not enough to claim novelty for an idea or concept. The artistic product must originate with the author— be original in that sense—but it need not be novel. To qualify for protection under copyright laws, a creator must provide an embodiment in particulars, a unique expression of an idea that many might otherwise possess in a generalized way. In the case of patents, novelty is crucial, but here the inventor must supply a concretely practicable embodiment that shows precisely how the general idea may be put in practice. The concreteness of the creation qualifies it for protection, not the spiritual immateriality of the general idea.

Let me repeat, since so many fail to grasp it on one pass: a *patent* covers a practical insight reduced to practice—that is the trick of the thing, the hard part—and a *copyright* covers the unique, personal way of presenting something by a writer or an artist. A patent is closely linked to the inventor's concrete grasp of the distinctive advance he or she makes on the practical state of the relevant art. A copyright is very clearly linked to the personal subjectivity of the author. Here concreteness is all, and, as the legal theorist Wendy J. Gordon points out, this concreteness furnishes the necessary analogy between property rights in material things and property rights in highly personal expressions of ideas (copyrights) or concretely exercisable practices (patents).[14]

Finally, we must clarify the rationale of the emphasis of the laws on proof of novelty. Some think it irrational that two or more persons may come to substantially the same invention while filing for a patent a day apart. It is unfair, they say, to reward the one totally and deny the other totally.[15]

But this is to forget that it is characteristic of any extension of the rule of law into new territory—the Homestead Act, for example—to reward those who stake the first claim. This may not be a perfect system, but tradition has proved its workability. The law sets up a competition for the frequent provision of real benefits to the common good of the society. Since for this purpose novelty is prized, timing is of the essence. As Professor Gordon sharply puts it, "When several scientists are hot on some trail, a promise of exclusivity to the winner may be the only prize meaningful enough to keep the race from flagging."[16] While the law must be as fair as humanly and administratively possible, it cannot play the role of an omniscient judge. We await perfect justice in a different city.

Five Disputed Questions

Even in the midst of the most terrible civil war in history, Abraham Lincoln assiduously promoted both the Homestead Act and the Land Grant College Act and continually praised the patent and copyright clause, stressing the importance of practical intellect to the generation of the nation's wealth.[17] Considering the high importance that Lincoln attached to this issue, it is odd to discover the relative neglect of intellectual property by scholars and social philosophers. Although the literature is already vast—in the past decade, more work has appeared on "intellectual property" than on "property" in general—countless serious issues remain unresolved. For this reason, the American Enterprise Institute not long ago commissioned a short survey of yet unanswered questions, Robert P. Benko's *Protecting Intellectual Property Rights*.[18]

The necessary inquiries, Benko shows, cut across several different disciplines. Many historical questions have gone uninvestigated. The philosophical foundations of patents and copyrights stand in considerable confusion. Still unresolved are the economic aspects of these laws, both in precise economic concepts and in their empirical foundation. It goes without saying that lawyers argue about their foundations,

meaning, and implications. Very few political theo-
rists have given to patents and copyrights anything
like the importance that Lincoln attaches to them.
Lincoln saw that the free society must open up economic opportunity to all, especially at the bottom, and
that for this purpose, public encouragement for invention and discovery is critical. Few other thinkers
have seen in these laws a crucial foundation of the
free society as Lincoln did.

Furthermore, one finds in the academy today
many who deny that there are such things as "rights,"
and even some who treat rights as they treat uni-
corns.[19] Similarly, one finds a surprising number who
attack even the concept of patent and copyright. A
surprising number of the latter actually have difficulties with the prior concept, property rights. They
find property rights too "conservative" and impli-
cated in something they affect to despise: "possessive individualism."[20] Others dislike the seeming
anomaly of granting "temporary monopolies" and
thus stigmatize patents and copyrights with the con-
tempt traditionally attached to monopolies.

This, of course, is a terminological mistake. *Monopoly* belongs to the language of domination over
competition, but *copyright* belongs to the language of
private property and establishes a right to enter into
markets. The point of a monopoly is to extinguish
competition, but the point of protecting the copyright
of authors is to ignite competition. The recognition
of copyright increases the number of competitors; its
aim is the opposite of monopoly.[21]

Again, while some hate the lack of competition
that inheres in what they improperly call "temporary

monopolies," others would prefer, at least with regard to intellectual achievements, an altogether non-
competitive world. Some even prefer a world of common ownership.[22] (This appeal to ownership shows
that they, too, are thinking of a "property" right, not
a "monopoly.") These critics further forget that existing patents and copyrights often inspire new rounds
of competition to "go around" the existing claims,
with the hope of launching more successful creations.
This is especially true in medical and pharmaceutical
research.[23] Patents and copyrights do not end competition; often, their success inspires it in surround-
ing areas.

Finally, truly serious practical problems in the
field of patents and copyrights today arise in three
areas: first, the search for international protections
for intellectual property; second, the search for protection in the new environment of electronic and digi-
tal communications; and, third, moral qualms about
the awe-inspiring fields of genetics and biogenetics.

Regarding international law, I offer two remarks.
Most nations have had no Lincoln to clarify their
thinking about the central role of intellectual property in the creation of wealth. In many countries,
therefore, basic philosophical clarity is lacking. Moreover, even where such clarity is achieved, the institu-
tional and administrative requirements for staffing a
national patent and copyright office are beyond the
abilities of many nations. A large number of international institutions must be confronted (the World Intellectual Property Organization, World Trade Organization, and UNESCO, not to mention bilateral and
multilateral boards and commissions), and finding

one's way through that minefield is not easy. (It takes
more than a village—it takes hundreds of thousands
of dollars and many thousands of man hours—to win
an international patent today.) While most of the political debate and jostling on the subject focus on WTO
rules, enforcement proceedings, bilateral treaties, and
jaw-boning, these are really just manifestations of the
lack of consensus on the foundations of intellectual
property. More sharply put: if developing and non-
Western nations *did* appreciate the importance of patents and copyright, then international conventions
and enforcement would be straightforward—as rou-
tine as international enforcement of business con-
tracts, tangible property rights, and maritime law,
where there is already consensus.

Regarding the grievous problems for patents and
copyrights brought on by new modes of communi-
cation, I make but one observation. Since the printing press occasioned the emergence of copyright laws
in the first place, wouldn't it be ironic if a new communications revolution—this time in electronics—
rendered copyrights unprotectable?[24] For myself, I
propose a simple rule: never bet against the survival
of the book, the printed word, and the copyright.

Again, some people say that 50 percent of the
computer software put into individual work stations
is already being copied in violation of copyrights. (In
borrowing a program from friends, is there anyone
without sin?) But, as Philip E. Ross has recently
shown, in the war between inventors seeking to protect their intellectual property and "pirates" strug-
gling to swipe it, the battle is constantly shifting fronts.
Two broad strategies for combating piracy are shap-

ing up: one technological, the other legislative. Both hardware and software are being developed that can "read" copyright signatures to block illegitimate copying and "encrypt" envelopes that must be decoded before use. On the other front, legislators have already imposed a "royalty tax" on copying materials and recording devices at the point of sale to compensate those who will lose profits from their use.[25] With appropriate skepticism about their practicality, we can anticipate other such legislative initiatives in the future.

Finally, profound philosophical and theological questions are also raised by patenting in genetics and biogenetics, and I must say a few words on these matters because of their urgency.

But Isn't Genetics Different?

The prospect of "patents on body parts" (that is the way discussion of genetics is amateurishly put) seems to arouse revulsion, for example, in a writer whose article as an editor I once published.[26] As a philosopher and theologian, however, I have come to have a higher professional regard than I used to for what my colleague James Q. Wilson calls "the moral sentiments,"[27] including spontaneous revulsion. For a long time, I resisted formulating philosophical views rooted in the sentiments, and I still deplore people's saying, "I *feel* that" instead of "I *judge* that." Nowadays, however, since to be politically correct we are supposed to make ourselves believe a dozen revolting things before breakfast, we have all learned to take spontaneous feelings more seriously than we used to. Revulsion is often reason's best defense.

True enough, medical inventors in our time have developed magnificent artificial substitutes to replace certain "body parts" after our original organs and limbs give out, enabling us to live longer and better lives. When Pope John Paul II broke his hip in 1994, for example, a partial hip replacement was available for him.

In genetics and biogenetics, however, something rather different is in question. Nobody is talking about physical body parts such as arms, legs, and kidneys but about identifying and isolating components of our genetic makeup. This "something different" is so intimately bound up with our personal identity that we are bound to approach it with awe, not a little trembling, and caution. Research in this area arouses deep but obscure feelings. There is strong resistance to the idea of patenting important elements of the human person—characteristics that are, as it were, right at the inner trunk of the tree of family traits that shape each of us. How can it be right to patent something so intimate, so potent, and so surrounded with danger? Genetic research would seem to give human beings power over the genetic makeup of future generations. Isn't that too awesome a power to give to humans?

Despite such fears, practically everyone agrees that there can be a good side to some genetic research. On the positive side, here is Pope John Paul II:

> Scientific progress such as that involving the genome is a credit to human reason, for man is called to be lord of creation, and it honors

the Creator, source of all life, who entrusted the human race with stewardship over the world.[28]

But what about the potential evils, the "Frankenstein" effects? Richard D. Land and C. Ben Mitchell mention several:[29] the creation of "transgenic animals," that is, human-altered creatures genetically engineered to serve as means to other ends;[30] the patenting of genetically engineered human beings;[31] and even the prospect of human embryos cloned for the sole purpose of "farming" their tissue for medical research.[32] The first of these cases, transgenic animals, disturbs some scholars, but others find it not much different from the use of genetics in altering plants. As for the other two—genetically engineered human beings and the cloning of embryos for "farming" purposes—they arouse profound moral doubts, even moral revulsion, in many.

Before we collapse all problems into these worst cases, however, it is useful first to distinguish among the many types of genetic research. Certain diseases and bodily vulnerabilities, it has long been known, are inherited, and the precise genes that result in these defects can now be isolated. At earlier stages in medical history, medical interventions to cure or to temper inherited diseases and other vulnerabilities have been regarded as ethically permissible, even admirable.

For healing such difficulties, for example, this new knowledge about genes and how to isolate them, although it has yet to cure anyone of a genetic disease, has opened up new possibilities for intervention. That intervention is more radical, it is true, but it does not alter the fundamental structure of the human person; its main goal, on the contrary, is to rectify abnormal deficiencies. The isolation of the gene causing sickle cell anemia, a grave blood disorder affecting more than 50,000 Americans (most of them African-American), has led to the development of a synthetic molecule that shows great promise in treating the inherited disease. Similar molecules may provide remedies for cystic fibrosis and other diseases.[33] The pope himself lauds this sort of genetic medicine:

> We can reasonably foresee that the whole genome sequencing will open new paths of research for therapeutic purposes. Thus the sick, to whom it was impossible to give proper treatment due to frequently hereditary pathologies, will be able to benefit from the treatment needed to improve their condition and possibly to cure them. By acting on the subject's unhealthy genes, it will also be possible to prevent the recurrence of genetic diseases and their transmission.[34]

Genetic research leading to pharmaceutical interventions of this type would seem, then, to fall within traditional ethical norms.

Morally serious people must soon develop a complete taxonomy of the types of genetic research and genetic interventions and the different sorts of ethical reflection each type might call for. The entire subject is new and arduous. The key point to be established for now is that there are different types of genetic research, each requiring its own proper form of ethical analysis. To speak of genetic research globally, without making important distinctions about kinds and specific differences, is a serious error. After we have considered the evidence, it is important for us to reach moral judgments early in this new field, but according to the ancient motto: *Festina lente* (hurry slowly).

We can never forget that medicine as practiced by two recent totalitarian regimes, Nazi and Communist, fell into grievously immoral uses. Such uses of medicine (or of scientific research more generally) need to be identified as early as possible and blocked in the body politic by appropriate checks and balances. But sinister uses—that is, *abuses*—of sound medicine should not be confused with beneficent uses. While the use to which genetic research is put must be subject to ethical judgment and command, the gaining of the required knowledge and the learning of the required practice would seem to be ethically good, analogous to the acquisition of practical knowledge in other areas of human inquiry.

For, in the timeless philosophy (*philosophia perennis*)[35] of the Western tradition, the human mind has as its natural good the raising and answering of all questions about everything, the complete fulfillment of the unlimited hunger to know. For me, this tradition was well expressed by my Jesuit teacher in Rome many years ago, Bernard Lonergan:

> Deep within us all, emergent when the noise
> of other appetites is stilled, there is a drive
> to know, to understand, to see why, to dis-

cover the reason, to find the cause, to explain. Just what is wanted, has many names.
In what precisely it consists, is a matter of
dispute. But the fact of inquiry is beyond
all doubt. It can absorb a man. It can keep
him for hours, day after day, year after year,
in the narrow prison of his study or his labo-
ratory. It can send him on dangerous voy-
ages of exploration. It can withdraw him
from other interests, other pursuits, other
pleasures, other achievements. It can fill his
waking thoughts, hide from him the world
of ordinary affairs, invade the very fabric of
his dreams. It can demand endless sacrifices
that are made without regret though there
is only the hope, never a certain promise, of
success. What better symbol could one find
for this obscure, exigent, imperious drive,
than a man, naked, running, excitedly cry-
ing, "I've got it"?[36]

Granted, then, that some forms of genetic research are morally sound, even imperative, even
while other forms may finally be judged to be evil,
why should we allow such knowledge to be patented?
Don't patents serve private interests rather than the
common good?

Does a Patent Regime Protect
Private Interests or Public Good?

On my way to answering this question, I hit a real
stumbling block in the words of an author from whom
I had learned much about intellectual property and,

indeed, about property rights of all kinds, Friedrich Hayek. In short, much to my initial surprise, Hayek *opposed* patents and copyrights:

> I doubt whether there exists a single great work of literature which we would not possess had the author been unable to obtain an exclusive copyright for it . . . .
>
> Similarly, recurrent re-examinations of the problem have not demonstrated that the obtainability of patents of invention actually enhances the flow of new technical knowledge rather than leading to wasteful concentration of research on problems whose solution in the near future can be foreseen and where, in consequence of the law, anyone who hits upon a solution a moment before the next gains the right to its exclusive use for a prolonged period.[37]

Hayek usually turns out to be right, so at first these sentences made me hesitate. After reflection, however, I found that I must part company with Hayek on this matter.

One alternative to a patent system is research that is kept secret—a regime of "trade secrets." There are thousands of such private and closely guarded trade secrets, the most famous perhaps being the formula for Coca-Cola. But the great advantage of a regime of patents over a regime of trade secrets is open publication. A patent is placed on the public record in precise detail; only that which is declared in public documents is protected. Ironically, therefore, a regime of patents makes publicly available the practical knowledge that a regime without patents often leaves secret and inaccessible and thereby expands the realm of publicly accessible science.[38] Further, it adds to the drive to inquire the incentive to better one's condition. This, as Lincoln saw, is an unstoppable combination.

The other alternative to a regime of patents was suggested by Hayek, who argued that the case for copyright "must rest almost entirely on the circumstance that such exceedingly useful works as encyclopaedias, dictionaries, textbooks and other works of reference could not be produced if, once they existed, they could freely be reproduced."[39] (Take, for instance, the fact that Noah Webster was one of the great early defenders of copyrights in the United States.) Except for that case, and contrary to his views on other forms of property, Hayek seemed to approve of common ownership of intellectual property.

Yet a regime of common ownership, often advanced as fulfilling the ideal of equality, would impose a cruel inequality on creators and inventors. These socially valuable persons would be expected to bear the costs in time, effort, financial investment, and personal sacrifice necessary to produce their creations, while all others would be freeloaders. Nations that have protected patents and copyrights, experience shows, have seen an explosion of invention and discovery far beyond anything achieved under nonpatent regimes. Although the Soviet regime made enormous investments in education, scientific research, and technological experimentation and although it produced some real successes, it lagged far behind in advancing the public good of its citizens and produced very little by way of practical invention for the common good.

While recognizing that intellectual property rights set certain temporary limits on consumption (by licensing the number of producers), I believe that withholding intellectual property rights limits production far more drastically, as the case of the Soviet Union clearly shows. This leads to the decisive point: how can anything be consumed if it has yet to be produced, and how can it be produced if there is no incentive for inventing it and bringing it to market?[40] Moreover, as Edmund W. Kitch points out in a remarkable paper, the fact that invention is treated as a property right—like a prospector's right in mining—establishes a market mechanism that gives clear signals about which inventions to bring forth first. Here, as elsewhere, these market signals greatly improve the efficiency of inventiveness[41] and call forth extraordinary efforts from ordinary people. Thus, well-designed regimes may bring forth better fruits than their citizens could produce unaided and thus stir strong feelings of gratitude among their citizens for the blessings they impart.

There is a second advantage to patent regimes: the expenses of research and the costs of applying for patents (and these have become formidable) are borne mostly by inventors. Of course, those companies that depend on a steady stream of a few successful inventions need to pass along the costs of their unsuccessful experiments; in this sense, they often "write off" these costs under research and development. Only if an invention actually succeeds in the market—and this happens in no more than a small fraction of cases—does its inventor recoup these expenses;[42] in fewer still does he make a profit. The costs of failure are by and large paid by luckless inventors, who may expend vast resources and come up empty—only to blaze the trail for those who follow in their footsteps and learn from their failures.

It is often suggested, finally, that the protection of intellectual property benefits the rich nations at the expense of third world countries. Why should rich "fat cats" prevent poor "copycats" from making cheap versions of certain pharmaceuticals or software programs? Or why, as James Boyle asks in a new book from Harvard University Press, should rich "first world" buyers be allowed to execute a "ferocious intellectual land grab" in the third world by enforcing rights to intellectual property?[43] This argument ignores the fact that those who are most victimized by the lack of intellectual property protection are the poor, as four considerations show.

First, when their best inventors and most creative minds migrate to countries where patent and copyright laws hold sway (like the many Russians now working in the American computer industry), nations without such protection suffer brain drain. Second, venture capital is desperately needed in the developing world, but the absence of intellectual property laws scares away venture capital—and jobs. Third, without patent and copyright protection, it is unlikely that multinationals will set up shop in a particular country; yet multinationals tend to bring with them more benefits, more humane treatment, and greater opportunity than are usually found in local sweat-

shops.[44] Fourth, without the protection of intellectual property rights, indigenous industries are unlikely to grow into multinational income producers
and large-scale employers of the sort their nations
need.

Conclusion

Sound public policy since at least the time of
Aristotle's *Nicomachean Ethics* has clung to a forthright
maxim, verified in practice over and over again: "If
you want more of something, reward it; if you want
less of something, punish it."[45] Regimes without patents penalize inventors and reward freeloaders.
Patent regimes recognize the right of inventors and
authors to the fruit of their own labors as a right in
common law. They do so because this right serves
the common good by stimulating useful inventions
and creative works from which a grateful public benefits. Far from protecting private interests at the expense of the common good, patent protection advances the common good by means of private interests. The common good is the end; private interest is
the means. Finally, experience shows that a patent
regime serves the common good better than any
known alternative.

The Jewish and Christian Bible, Abraham
Lincoln's favorite book, taught him that it is often
among the humblest things of this world that the
greatest blessings lie hid; and that it is among things
disdained and held in low esteem, among things overlooked and undervalued, that the greatest treasures
often lie. Lincoln put this beautifully: "All nature is

a wholly unexplored mine." Thus, patent and copyright laws, seemingly minor and humble instruments of liberty, were celebrated as never before by that both humblest and greatest president of the United States.

This lowly constitutional principle, one of the half-dozen most decisive advances in the history of liberty, gives incentive to millions to look again at the humble things around them, to discern the secrets the Creator has hidden from eternity for the benefit of all his people, if only the bold, the persevering, and the diligent will strain to uncover them.

Notes

1. Abraham Lincoln, "Lecture on Discoveries and Inventions," Jacksonville, Illinois, February 11, 1859, in *Speeches and Writings: 1859–1865* (Washington, D.C.: Library of America, 1989), p. 4.

2. It is interesting that Lincoln emphasizes the role of social habit in the dynamic of economic growth. For two recent works that empirically explore the role of such habits in economic success, see Francis Fukuyama, *Trust: The Social Virtues and the Creation of Prosperity* (New York: Free Press, 1995), pp. 43–48; and Thomas Sowell, *Migrations and Cultures: A World View* (New York: Basic Books, 1996), pp. 371–91.

3. The constitutional scholar Robert Goldwin underscores Lincoln's point:

> Lincoln made a helpful distinction. Genius has its own fire. The desire to decipher the mysteries of nature and of nature's laws, to make something that has never before existed, to say what has never before been said—these have a compelling power of their own. The love of wisdom or knowledge or understanding is, in a significant way, nonpolitical, nonsocietal. Its motivation is internal. It cannot be originated by constitutional provisions, no matter how skillfully drawn and implemented. But it can be fueled—encouraged, nurtured, protected, rewarded, and thus enhanced.

Genius, the power and originality of mind
that produces new thought, new understanding,
new inventions, has its own "fire" that society
at-large cannot plan, schedule, or produce. It
ignites, happily, in unpredictable persons, times,
and places, and when it does it is an individual
and private matter.

But societies need such innovative genius;
they neglect it at the risk of their own impover-
ishment. What the framers understood, and
what Lincoln's sentence illuminates so well, is
that the best that society at-large can do is provide more fuel for the fire of genius.

*Why Blacks, Women, and Jews Are Not Mentioned in the Con-
stitution, and Other Unorthodox Views* (Washington, D.C.:
AEI Press, 1990), p. 40.

4. See Fred Warshofsky, *The Patent Wars: The Battle to
Own the World's Technology* (New York: John Wiley & Sons,
Inc., 1994), p. 8.

5. See Thomas Jefferson, "A Summary View of the
Rights of British America," in Thomas Jefferson, *Writings*
(Washington, D.C.: Library of America, 1984), p. 122.

6. The pope adds:

The modern *business economy* has positive aspects. Its basis is human freedom exercised in
the economic field, just as it is exercised in many
other fields . . . and like every other sector, it
includes the right to freedom, as well as the duty
of making responsible use of freedom.

Pope John Paul II, *Centesimus Annus* (Washington, D.C.:
United States Catholic Conference, 1991), no. 32. For an
extended treatment of this encyclical, see my *Catholic Ethic
and the Spirit of Capitalism* (New York: Free Press, 1993),
pp. 114–43; and Richard John Neuhaus, *Doing Well and
Doing Good* (New York: Doubleday, 1992).

7. *Centesimus Annus*, no. 32.

8. There are now more than 1 billion Catholics, more than half in the third world. Note also the *political* contributions of the American experiment to the thought of Pope John Paul II:

> Pope Leo XIII was aware of the need for a sound *theory of the State* in order to ensure the normal development of man's spiritual and temporal activities, both of which are indispensable. For this reason, in one passage of *Rerum Novarum* [1891] he presents the organization of society according to the three powers—legislative, executive and judicial—, something which at the time represented a novelty in Church teaching. Such an ordering reflects a realistic vision of man's social nature, which calls for legislation capable of protecting the freedom of all. To that end, it is preferable that each power be balanced by other powers and by other spheres of responsibility which keep it within proper bounds. This is the principle of the "rule of law," in which the law is sovereign, and not the arbitrary will of individuals. [Ibid., p. 86]

See Russell Hittinger, "The Pope and the Liberal State," *First Things* (December 1992), pp. 33–41.

9. Warshofsky, *Patent Wars*, p. 3.

10. For the history of these events, consult Karl Fenning, "The Origin of the Patent and Copyright Clause of the Constitution," *Georgetown Law Journal*, 1921, pp. 109–17. For the earlier history of patent and copyright law, see Paul Goldstein, *Copyright's Highway: The Law and Lore of Copyright from Gutenberg to the Celestial Jukebox* (New York: Hill and Wang, 1994), pp. 37–77. The first international agreements on patents and copyrights did not occur until much later—the Paris Convention of 1883 and the Berne Convention of 1886. For more on the history of these laws, see William P. Kingston, *The Political Economy of Innova-*

tion (The Hague: Martinus Nijhuff Publishers, 1984), pp. 100–104. See also Arthur R. Miller and Michael H. Davis, *Intellectual Property: Patents, Trademarks and Copyright* (St. Paul, Minn.: West Publishing Co., 1983), esp. chaps. 1 and 10.

11. Concerning patents and copyrights, James Madison writes in *The Federalist Papers* No. 43 (New York: New American Library, 1961):

> The utility of this power will scarcely be questioned. The copyright of authors has been solemnly adjudged in Great Britain to be a right at Common Law. The right to useful inventions seems with equal reason to belong to the inventors. The public good fully coincides in both cases with the claims of individuals. [pp. 271–72]

12. See Goldstein, *Copyright's Highway*, pp. 9–10.

13. See "Are Patents and Copyrights Morally Justified? The Philosophy of Property Rights and Ideal Objects," *Harvard Journal of Law and Public Policy*, vol. 13 (1989), pp. 817–65. As Palmer puts it, "Intellectual property rights are rights in ideal objects, which are distinguished from the material substrata in which they are instantiated," p. 818.

14. Wendy J. Gordon, "An Inquiry into the Merits of Copyright: The Challenges of Consistency, Consent, and Encouragement Theory," *Stanford Law Review*, vol. 41 (1989), pp. 1365–1477.

15. See Palmer, "Are Patents and Copyrights Morally Justified?" (p. 829), quoting William Leggett, the nineteenth-century Jacksonian editorialist: "If you assert an exclusive right to a particular idea, you cannot be sure that the very same idea did not at the same moment enter some other mind." Palmer calls this the "problem of simultaneous invention or discovery."

16. Gordon, "Inquiry into the Merits of Copyright," p. 1369.

17. See also Lincoln's "Address to the Wisconsin State Agricultural Society" (also of 1859), where he pays elo-

quent homage to the role invention plays in agriculture:

> I know of nothing so pleasant to the mind, as the discovery of anything which is at once *new* and *valuable*—nothing which so lightens and sweetens toil, as the hopeful pursuit of such discovery. And how vast, and how varied a field is agriculture, for such discovery. The mind, already trained to thought, in the country school, or higher school, cannot fail to find there an exhaustless source of profitable enjoyment. Every blade of grass is a study; and to produce two, where there was but one, is both a profit and a pleasure. And not grass alone; but soils, seeds, and seasons—hedges, ditches, and fences, draining, droughts, and irrigation—plowing, hoeing, and harrowing—reaping, moving, and threshing—saving crops, pests of crops, diseases of crops, and what will prevent or cure them—implements, utensils, and machines, their relative merits, and how to improve them—hogs, horses, and cattle—sheep, goats, and poultry—trees, shrubs, fruits, plants, and flowers—the thousand things of which these are specimens—each a world of study within itself.

Speeches and Writings: 1859-1865, pp. 99–100.

18.   Robert P. Benko, *Protecting Intellectual Property Rights: Issues and Controversies* (Washington, D.C.: American Enterprise Institute, 1987).

19.   As in the utilitarian tradition. See Palmer, "Are Patents and Copyrights Morally Justified?" pp. 820, 849–51.

20.   Gordon mentions the philosopher Alan Ryan in this regard. See Gordon, "An Inquiry into the Merits of Copyrights," p. 1345. For Ryan, see *The Political Theory of Property* (Oxford: Blackwell, 1984), pp. 163–64. For the urtext of this left-wing term, see C. B. Macpherson, *The Political Theory of Possessive Individualism* (Oxford:

Clarendon Press, 1962). Many who affect to despise the concept practice it.

21. As my AEI colleague Christopher DeMuth has emphasized to me, it is a confusion to call patents and copyrights "monopolies," because monopoly depends on conditions of market supply and demand: a monopoly is a good supplied by a single supplier *that has no close substitutes in use*. Thus, a patent or copyright *may* confer monopoly pricing power—but so may a property right in something tangible, such as a strategically located parcel of land. Moreover, a patent or copyright confers no monopoly where there are satisfactory substitutes for the new invention or writing. In other words, both "intellectual" and "tangible" property rights may lead to monopoly, but the purpose (and general effect) of those rights is to promote rather than to restrict competition and economic output.

22. See "Are Patents and Copyrights Morally Justified?" Palmer, pp. 860–61.

23. In his recent book, *The Heroic Enterprise*, John Hood tells the story of Dr. Raymond Damadian, the inventor of the magnetic resonance imaging (MRI) device, one of the most important medical advances of the past few decades whose primary use is to find cancers that otherwise might go undiagnosed for years:

> Damadian began working on the idea in 1970 and, with a colleague, began testing the technology on rats at a private research lab in Pittsburgh. Proving the concept to be workable, Damadian obtained a patent in 1974 and by 1977 had tested an MRI scanner on a human being. The following year, Damadian and his coworkers started FONAR Corporation to manufacture MRI scanners. By 1982 large domestic and foreign companies decided the concept made sense and began introducing their own MRI products

despite Damadian's patent. Over the next few years, even as FONAR pursued legal action, the company continued to refine MRI technology, generating more than 80 percent of all the innovations in the industry and securing another twenty patents. But every innovation the company introduced was promptly copied by its largest competitors . . . . Even though patents protect innovative companies from having their ideas stolen by others, they do not protect these firms from competition. In virtually every case where a drug has been introduced to treat a medical condition, alternative treatments for that condition exist, sometimes including other patented drugs.

The Heroic Enterprise: Business and the Common Good (New York: Free Press, 1996), p. 100.

24. See Goldstein, *Copyright's Highway*, chaps. 4 and 6, for the complexity of the new problems.

25. See Philip E. Ross, "Cops versus Robbers in Cyberspace," *Forbes*, September 9, 1996, pp. 134–39. See also Goldstein, *Copyright's Highway*, pp. 158–64, on the history behind the Audio Home Recording Act of 1992. Wendy J. Gordon notes an important psychological difference that often attends theft of intellectual property:

One need climb no fences to make copies of intellectual products . . . . One knows one is doing something wrong when one tries to sneak into a neighbor's house or pick the lock of another's automobile; it may not seem so obviously wrong to tape a musical recording or duplicate a computer program that is already in hand. In addition, an act of copying seems to harm no one. There is no perceptible loss, no shattered lock or broken fencepost, no blood, not even a psychological sense of trespass.

Gordon, "Inquiry into the Merits of Copyright," p. 1346.

26. See Andrew Kimbrell, "Patents Encroach upon the Body," *Crisis*, May 1993, pp. 43–48. Kimbrell's book, *The Human Body Shop* (San Francisco: HarperCollins, 1993), develops his argument at length.

27. See Wilson's book, *The Moral Sense* (New York: Free Press, 1993) for his full treatment of the moral sentiments, an emphasis given prominence by the Scottish Enlightenment.

28. Pope John Paul II, "Address to Pontifical Academy of Sciences," *L'Osservatore Romano*, November 1994, p. 3.

29. The argument on the moral status of biogenetic experimentation and gene patenting is well underway. In May of 1996, for example, the American Enterprise Institute held a day-long conference, "The Ethics of Gene Patenting." For Richard D. Land and Ben Mitchell, see "Patenting Life: No," *First Things* (May 1996), pp. 20–22. In the same issue, Ted Peters weighs in on the other side with "Patenting Life: Yes," pp. 18–19. Both arguments were responding to a May 18, 1995, press conference held by a group of religious leaders in Washington, D.C. The conference called for a ban on patenting human genes and genetically engineered animals. Led by the naturalist Jeremy Rifkin, those endorsing the "Joint Appeal against Human and Animal Patenting" included Rabbi Saperstein (director of the Religious Action Center of Reform Judaism); Abdurahman Alamoudi (executive director of the American Muslim Council); and Wesley Granberg Michaelson (secretary general of the Reformed Church in America). Rifken summed up the appeal: "By turning life into patented inventions, the government drains life of its intrinsic nature and sacred value." For an extremely clear presentation of the case for the moral legitimacy of gene patents, see Baruch A. Brody, "On Patenting Transgenic Animals," *The Ag Bioethics Forum*, vol. 7, no. 2 (November 1995). Brody argues that opposition to gene patenting tends to invest nature with a sacredness at odds

with Jewish and Christian teaching on man's dominion over nature.

30. Land and Mitchell do not object in their article in *First Things* to the creation of such creatures as the "oncomouse"—a mouse genetically engineered to carry a cancer gene useful for human cancer research—but do object to patenting it: "While animal ownership per se is morally acceptable, patenting animals represents an abuse of the notion of ownership, and more importantly of ownership rights." Land and Mitchell, "Patenting Life: No," p. 20. Elsewhere, however, Land seemingly rejects the genetic engineering itself by describing "altering life forms, creating new life forms, as a revolt against the sovereignty of God and an attempt to be God." Quoted in Peters, "Patenting Life: Yes," p. 19. What often disguises itself as an antipatenting position is in reality a profound distrust of man's prometheanism.

31. Although Land and Mitchell admit that "whole human beings have not been patented," they are troubled by the fact that "by September 4, 1993, the National Institutes of Health had filed for patents on 6,122 gene fragments. Although patenting of 'gene fragments of unknown biological function' is presently disallowed, who knows what the future holds?" Land and Mitchell, "Patenting Life: No," p. 20.

32. On embryo cloning, the Italian philosopher Rocco Buttiglione writes:

> The real issue is not embryo cloning; the issue has to do with love, responsibility and family. Only in this way can the child establish close ties—that mix of love and authority that is moral education—which will enable him to become a mature, responsible individual in a free society. That kind of person cannot be "produced" in a laboratory. If we try to "produce" a child as if he were a machine, or a commodity on an as-

sembly line, we do not respect his dignity.

"Immoral Clones: A Vatican View," *New Perspectives Quarterly*, vol. 3, no.1 (Winter 1994).

33. See "Advance Reported on Sickle Cell Anemia," *New York Times*, September 6, 1996.

34. Pope John Paul II, "Address to Pontifical Academy of Sciences," p. 3.

35. Walter Lippmann calls this the "public philosophy." See his book, *The Public Philosophy* (Rutgers, N.J.: Transaction Publishers, 1989). See also the work of Jacques Maritain, in particular, *The Degrees of Knowledge*, ed. R. McInerny, trans. G. Phelan (Notre Dame, Ind.: University of Notre Dame Press, 1996).

36. Bernard Lonergan, *Insight: A Study of Human Understanding* (New York: Longmans, 1957), p. 4.

37. Friedrich von Hayek, *The Fatal Conceit: The Errors of Socialism*, ed. W. W. Bartley III (Chicago: University of Chicago Press, 1989), pp. 36–37.

38. This is why I find it difficult to understand this passage from the Pope John Paul II's "Address to Pontifical Academy of Sciences":

> On this subject, we rejoice that numerous researchers have refused to allow discoveries made about the genome to be patented. Since the human body is not an object that can be disposed of at will, the results of research should be made available to the whole scientific community and cannot be the property of a small group. [p. 3]

It is only fair to note that Hayek and the pope agree on this point. So far as I can discover, however, the Vatican has not otherwise addressed the general role of patents in serving the common good.

39. Hayek, *The Fatal Conceit*, p. 22.

40. See Peter Huber, "Private Property," a review of James Boyle, *Shamans, Software and Spleens, New York Times Book Review,* September 22, 1996, p. 18.

41. Edmund W. Kitch, "The Nature and Function of the Patent System," *Journal of Law and Economics,* vol. 20 (October 1977), pp. 265–90.

42. Take, for example, the pharmaceutical industry, where 18.8 percent of sales is devoted to "R&D"—the odds of developing a useful new drug from original conception to marketplace delivery are 1 in 5,000. The process requires an average investment of $450 million, fifty disciplines, and twelve to fifteen years of work. See "Protecting Intellectual Property in the Pharmaceutical Industry—A Critical Key to Worldwide Health and Economic Development" (unpublished manuscript, 1996); see also chap. 6 of Hood, *The Heroic Enterprise,* pp. 96–129.

43. Quoted in Huber, "Private Property," p. 18.

44. For a perhaps surprising recognition of the benefits of investment by multinational corporations for developing nations, see John Kenneth Galbraith, "The Defense of the Multinational Company," *Harvard Business Review* (March–April 1979), pp. 83–93. See more recently, Irwin M. Stelzer, "Nice Town, Shantytown," *Weekly Standard,* September 16, 1996, pp. 18–20. See also chap. 8 of my book *Business as a Calling: Work and the Examined Life* (New York: Free Press, 1996), pp. 160–75. On the role of patent protection in the developing world, see Edmund W. Kitch, "The Patent Policy of Developing Countries," *UCLA Pacific Basin Law Journal,* vol. 13, 1994, pp. 166–78.

45. As Aristotle put it:

Moral excellence is concerned with pleasures and pains; it is on account of the pleasure that we do bad things, and on account of the pain that we abstain from noble ones. Hence we ought to have been brought up in a particular way from our very youth . . . so as both to de-

light in and to be pained by the things we ought;
for this is the right education.

Nicomachean Ethics, trans. W. D. Ross, book II, chap. 3 in
The Basic Works of Aristotle, ed. Richard McKeon (New York:
Random House, 1941), p. 954.

About the Author

MICHAEL NOVAK, the Templeton laureate, holds the George Frederick Jewett Chair in Religion, Philosophy, and Public Policy at the American Enterprise Institute. He is also AEI's director of social and political studies. In 1986, Mr. Novak headed the U.S. delegation to the Conference on Security and Cooperation in Europe. In 1981 and 1982, he led the U.S. delegation to the United Nations Human Rights Commission in Geneva. In 1994, Mr. Novak won the Templeton Prize for Progress in Religion, the Wilhelm Weber Prize, and the International Award of the Institution for World Capitalism. The author of more than twenty-five books, he is also a cofounder and former publisher of *Crisis* and has been a columnist for both *National Review* and *Forbes*.